ICONS

PARIS STYLE
VOL. II

PARIS

Exteriors Interiors

STYLE

Details

EDITOR **Angelika Taschen**

VOL. II

TASCHEN

HONG KONG KÖLN LONDON LOS ANGELES MADRID PARIS TOKYO

Front Cover: Paris combines the traditional and the modern – as in this opulent salon on Boulevard Haussmann.
Couverture : À Paris, l'ancien et le moderne cohabitent avec bonheur – par exemple dans ce salon du boulevard Haussmann.
Umschlagvorderseite: Paris verbindet Tradition und Moderne – wie in diesem mondänen Salon am Boulevard Haussmann.

Back Cover: The Krzentowskis' apartment has a view of two emblems of the city at once – the Seine and the Eiffel Tower.
Dos de Couverture : L'appartement des Krzentowski avec vue sur la Seine et la tour Eiffel, deux emblèmes de la ville.
Umschlagrückseite: Von der Wohnung der Krzentowskis sieht man gleich zwei Wahrzeichen – die Seine und den Eiffelturm.

Also available from TASCHEN:

New Paris Interiors
Hardcover 24 x 31.6 cm, 300 pages
ISBN 978-3-8365-0250-4 (Edition with English and German cover)
ISBN 978-3-8365-0252-8 (Edition with French Cover)

To stay informed about upcoming TASCHEN titles, please request our magazine at
www.taschen.com/magazine or write to TASCHEN, Hohenzollernring 53, D-50672 Cologne,
Germany, contact@taschen.com, Fax: +49-221-254919. We will be happy to send you
a free copy of our magazine which is filled with information about all of our books.

© 2009 TASCHEN GmbH
Hohenzollernring 53, D-50672 Köln
www.taschen.com

© 2009 VG Bild-Kunst, Bonn for the works of Bernard Dufour, Ange Leccia, Hubert Le Gall,
Jean Prouvé and Roger Tallon.
© 2009 for the works of Charles and Ray Eames: Eames Office, Venice, CA, www.eamesoffice.com.

Concept, layout and editing by Angelika Taschen, Berlin
General project management by Stephanie Paas, Cologne
Texts by Christiane Reiter, Hamburg
Lithography by Thomas Grell, Cologne
English translation by John Sykes, Cologne
French translation by Michèle Schreyer, Cologne

Printed in Italy
ISBN 978-3-8365-1505-4

CONTENTS SOMMAIRE INHALT

"What makes Paris so magical?" the writer Kurt Tucholsky once asked. "The architecture? The silvery air? The fashion? The women? Champagne? All these things together?" The architecture – that is what most people think of first when they think about the phenomenon that is Paris. From the Eiffel Tower, which was originally intended to stand for only 20 years but has been reaching for the sky for a good 120 years now, to the romantic Pont des Arts that spans the Seine behind the Louvre, and Haussmann's perfectly proportioned buildings, which have put their stamp on the face of most arrondissements since the 19th century: this architecture lends Paris splendour, glamour and a certain magnificence. And as far as the silvery shimmer in the air, elegant women wearing haute couture and the sparkling champagne are concerned, many would agree with Tucholsky. However, in order to describe the character of Paris today, it is necessary to add in a further factor that

THE MAGIC OF PARIS

L'écrivain allemand Kurt Tucholsky qui y a vécu quelques années s'est demandé ce qui fait la magie de Paris : « L'architecture ? L'air argenté ? La mode ? Les femmes ? Le champagne ? Tout cela à la fois ? » L'architecture est sans doute la première chose qui vient à l'esprit de la plupart des gens qui tentent d'analyser le phénomène. Il suffit d'évoquer la tour Eiffel, construite pour durer vingt ans à l'origine et qui se dresse depuis plus de 120 ans dans le ciel de Paris, ou le romantique Pont des Arts qui traverse la Seine derrière le Louvre et les bâtiments aux proportions parfaites du baron Haussmann, qui marquent depuis le 19ᵉ siècle le visage de la plupart des arrondissements. L'architecture de ses bâtiments donne de l'éclat à la ville, du glamour, un air grandiose. Pour ce qui est de l'air argenté, des vêtements Haute Couture portés par des femmes élégantes et du champagne, Tucholsky est dans le vrai – néanmoins celui qui veut décrire aujourd'hui le caractère de la capitale doit prendre aussi en considération un élément qui a commencé

»Worin besteht der Zauber von Paris?«, fragte Kurt Tucholsky einmal. »In der Architektur? In der silbrigen Luft? In der Mode? In den Frauen? Im Sekt? In all dem zusammen?« Die Architektur – sie kommt wohl den meisten Menschen zuerst in den Sinn, wenn sie dem Phänomen Paris nachspüren. Vom Eiffelturm, der ursprünglich nur 20 Jahre stehen sollte, mittlerweile aber schon gut 120 Jahre lang in den Himmel ragt, über die romantische Brücke Pont des Arts, die hinter dem Louvre die Seine überspannt, bis zu den perfekt proportionierten Haussmann-Gebäuden, die seit dem 19. Jahrhundert das Gesicht der meisten Arrondissements prägen: Die Architektur verleiht Paris Glanz, Glamour und etwas Grandioses. Auch in puncto silbrig schimmernder Luft, Haute Couture bei eleganten Frauen und perlendem Champagner mag man Tucholsky recht geben – doch wer heute das Wesen und den Charakter von Paris beschreiben möchte, muss einen Faktor hinzufügen, der erst nach Tucholskys Zeiten ebenfalls eine

began to play a part after Tucholsky's era, the 1920s: the city's feeling for design and contemporary art. Paris is no longer a place where people mainly follow the French classical tradition and live in old buildings that are certainly magnificent, but always resemble each other. In the 21st century Paris prefers to take its cue all from contemporary architecture and design. Architects, designers, interior designers, artists and of course connoisseurs of art and collectors from all over the world live and work together in close proximity here; they showcase classics of French 20th-century design as well as international contemporary art, create spectacular showrooms in historic buildings or convert apartments full of nooks and crannies into lofts with breathtaking views. They combine the traditional beauty of the city with the latest ideas, give a new accent to French flair and find ever-new interpretations of its legendary chic style – this is the magic of Paris.

à jouer un rôle après l'époque de l'écrivain : le sens du design et de l'art contemporain.

Paris n'est plus un endroit dédié au style classique français et où l'on habite dans des constructions anciennes superbes soit, mais qui se ressemblent pratiquement toutes. Au 21ᵉ siècle, la ville s'oriente surtout sur l'architecture et le design contemporains. Ici des architectes, des architectes d'intérieur, des designers, des artistes et bien sûr aussi des amateurs d'art et des collectionneurs du monde entier vivent côte à côte, mettant en scène des classiques du design français du 20ᵉ siècle aussi bien que des œuvres de l'art contemporain international, créant de spectaculaires show-rooms dans des bâtiments historiques ou transformant des appartements tout en coins et recoins en lofts offrant une vue prodigieuse sur la ville. Ils marient la beauté traditionnelle de la capitale aux idées actuelles, donnent une note innovante au goût français et interprètent de manière toujours originale le chic légendaire – voilà ce qui fait la magie de Paris.

Rolle zu spielen begann: den Sinn der Stadt für Design und zeitgenössische Kunst.

Paris ist kein Ort mehr, wo man sich hauptsächlich an der französischen Klassik orientiert und in durchaus prachtvollen, aber immer ähnlichen Altbauten wohnt. Paris orientiert sich mit dem 21. Jahrhundert inzwischen vor allem an zeitgenössischer Architektur und Design. Hier leben und arbeiten Architekten, Innenausstatter, Designer, Künstler und natürlich auch Kunstkenner und Sammler aus aller Welt eng zusammen, setzen französische Designklassiker des 20. Jahrhunderts ebenso wie internationale Gegenwartskunst in Szene, entwerfen in historischen Häusern spektakuläre Showrooms oder verwandeln verwinkelte Wohnungen in Lofts mit atemberaubender Aussicht. Sie verbinden die traditionelle Schönheit der Stadt mit aktuellen Ideen, verleihen dem französischen Flair eine neue Note und interpretieren den legendären Chic immer wieder neu – darin besteht der Zauber von Paris.

"… one always thinks of painters, as if Paris had adapted to the colours of famous palettes…"

Max Frisch, *Sketchbook 1946–1949*

« … on pense toujours aux peintres, comme si Paris s'était adaptée aux couleurs de célèbres palettes…»

Max Frisch, *Journal 1946–1949*

»… man denkt immer an Maler, so, als hätte sich Paris den Farben berühmter Paletten angepasst …«

Max Frisch, *Tagebuch 1946–1949*

EXTERIORS

Extérieurs   Aussichten

10/11 A mooring: the marina Port de l'Arsenal lies south of Place de la Bastille. *Bateaux au mouillage : le port de plaisance de l'Arsenal au sud de la place de la Bastille.* Ankerplatz: Südlich der Place de la Bastille liegt der Freizeithafen Port de l'Arsenal.

12/13 Play of light: around Place du Trocadéro the monumental side of Paris is on view. *Jeux de lumière : la place du Trocadéro et le visage monumental de Paris.* Lichtspiele: Rund um die Place du Trocadéro zeigt sich Paris von der monumentalen Seite.

14/15 An emblem: since 1889 the Eiffel Tower has soared 300 metres into the city sky. *Emblème : depuis 1889, la tour Eiffel haute de 300 mètres surplombe Paris.* Wahrzeichen: Seit 1889 ragt der Eiffelturm 300 Meter in den Himmel über der Stadt.

16/17 A sought-after address: Carine Roitfeld's apartment is close to the Hôtel des Invalides. *Une adresse très recherchée : l'appartement de Carine Roitfeld est situé à côté de l'Hôtel des Invalides.* Begehrte Adresse: Die Wohnung von Carine Roitfeld liegt nahe dem Hôtel des Invalides.

18/19 Highlights: from Cathy Vedovi's roof terrace the view extends as far as the Eiffel Tower. *Sommets : du toit-terrasse de Cathy Vedovi on aperçoit même la tour Eiffel.* Höhepunkte: Von Cathy Vedovis Dachterrasse reicht die Sicht bis zum Eiffelturm.

20/21 Living by the water: an apartment block directly on the quayside at Port de l'Arsenal. *Au bord de l'eau : un immeuble d'appartements sur le quai du Port de l'Arsenal.* Wohnen am Wasser: ein Apartmenthaus direkt am Kai des Port de l'Arsenal.

22/23 A retail palace: La Samaritaine on the Seine with its Art Deco façade. *La Samaritaine et sa façade Art déco au bord de la Seine.* Ein Einkaufstempel: das »La Samaritaine« an der Seine mit seiner Art-déco-Fassade.

24/25 A stroke of luck: from her apartment India Mahdavi has a view of the Paul Claudel Park. *Coup de chance : de son appartement, India Mahdavi voit le parc Paul Claudel.* Glücksgriff: India Mahdavi blickt von ihrem Apartment aus in den Paul-Claudel-Park.

26/27 Parisian splendour: 19th-century Haussmann façades on Square des Batignolles. *Splendeurs parisiennes : façades haussmanniennes du 19e siècle au square des Batignolles.* Pariser Pracht: Haussmann-Fassaden aus dem 19. Jahrhundert an der Square des Batignolles.

28/29 Philosopher: the monument to Jean-Jacques Rousseau on Place du Panthéon. *Hommage à Jean-Jacques Rousseau : le monument à sa mémoire sur la place du Panthéon.* Philosoph: das Denkmal von Jean-Jacques Rousseau auf der Place du Panthéon.

30/31 Good morning: "petit déjeuner" on the balcony of Hôtel Bourg Tibourg in the Marais. *Bonjour : petit-déjeuner sur le balcon de l'Hôtel Bourg Tibourg au Marais.* Guten Morgen: »Petit déjeuner« auf dem Balkon des Hôtel Bourg Tibourg im Marais.

32/33 A historic view: the Hôtel des Invalides was built 1671–1676 during Louis XIV's reign. *Face-à-face avec l'Histoire : l'Hôtel des Invalides (1671–1676) a été construit sous Louis XIV.* Geschichte im Visier: Das Hôtel des Invalides wurde 1671–1676 unter Ludwig XIV. erbaut.

34/35 Shining golden: the equestrian statue of Jeanne of Arc on Place des Pyramides. *L'éclat de l'or : la statue équestre de Jeanne d'Arc sur la place des Pyramides.* In goldenem Glanz: das Reiterstandbild der Jeanne d'Arc auf der Place des Pyramides.

36/37 The most beautiful square in Paris: Victor Hugo used to stroll across Place des Vosges. *La plus belle place de Paris : Victor Hugo aimait se promener sur la place des Vosges.* Der schönste Platz von Paris: Über die Place des Vosges flanierte einst Victor Hugo.

38/39 A walk by a palace: Maria de Medici's palais in the Jardin du Luxembourg. *Promenade : Marie de Médicis a fait construire le palais au Jardin du Luxembourg.* Spaziergang am Schloss: Das Palais im Jardin du Luxembourg gab Maria de Medici in Auftrag.

40/41 An elevated position: one of four bishops on the Visconti Fountain, Place Saint-Sulpice. *Digne : l'un des quatre évêques de la fontaine Visconti, place Saint-Sulpice.* Erhaben: eine von vier Bischofsfiguren des Visconti-Brunnens auf der Place Saint-Sulpice.

42/43 Bon appétit: the locals order bistro dishes at Au Bon Saint-Pourçain. *Bon appétit : Au Bon Saint Pourçain on peut déguster la cuisine française traditionnelle.* Bon appétit: Im »Au Bon Saint-Pourçain« bestellen Pariser Bistro-Gerichte.

44/45 At the heart of the Marais: a typically French bistro in Rue Vieille du Temple. *Au cœur du Marais : un bistrot typiquement français dans la rue Vieille du Temple.* Mitten im Marais: ein typisch französisches Bistro in der rue Vieille du Temple.

46/47 Film set: "The Wonderful World of Amélie" was filmed at this café in Pigalle. *Décor de cinéma : « Le fabuleux destin d'Amélie Poulain » a été tourné dans ce café à Pigalle.* Filmkulisse: Im »Café des Deux Moulins« in Pigalle wurde »Die fabelhafte Welt der Amélie« gedreht.

48/49 A work of art in glass: I. M. Pei's pyramid in the courtyard of the Louvre – seen from Café Marly. *Verre et métal : vue du Café Marly, la pyramide d'I. M. Pei dans la cour du Louvre.* Gläsernes Kunstwerk: I. M. Peis Pyramide im Hof des Louvre – vom Café Marly aus gesehen.

"Along the entire wall … were mirrors fitted between the marble panels, looking like doors opening into an infinite series of brightly lit halls…"

Émile Zola, *The Belly of Paris*

«…d'autres glaces, prises entre les plaques de marbre, mettaient des lacs de clarté, des portes qui semblaient s'ouvrir sur d'autres salles, à l'infini…»

Émile Zola, *Le ventre de Paris*

»Zwischen den Marmorplatten waren an der ganzen Wand Spiegel eingelassen. Helle Seen öffneten sich wie Türen bis ins Unendliche zu anderen Räumen …«

Émile Zola, *Der Bauch von Paris*

INTERIORS

Intérieurs   Einsichten

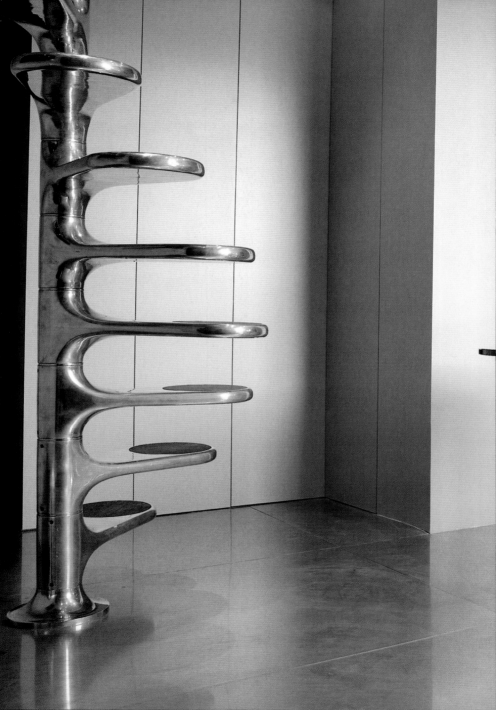

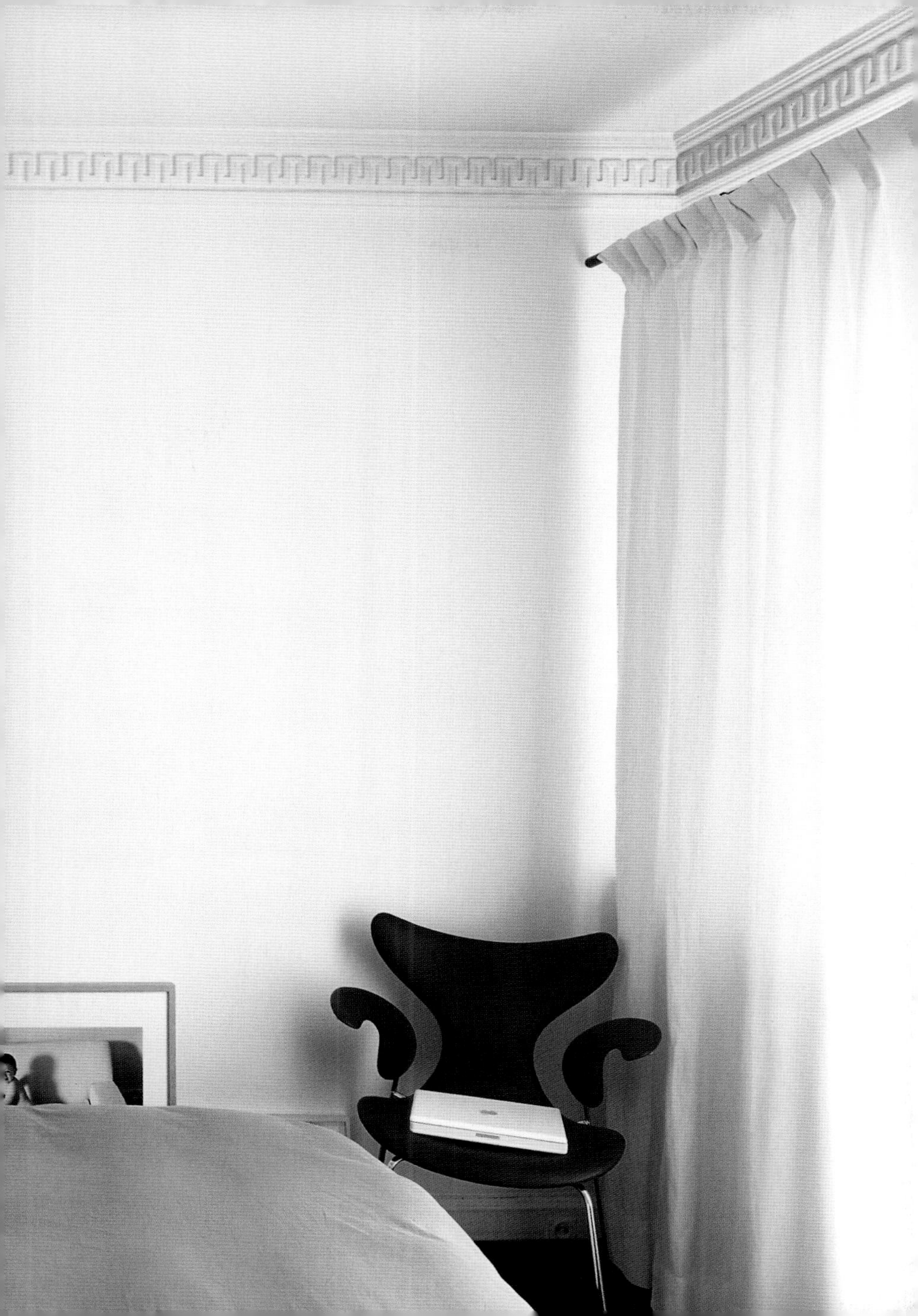

54/55 A glamorous apartment: Michael Coorengel & Jean-Pierre Calvagrac love opulence. *Glamour : Michael Coorengel & Jean-Pierre Calvagrac aiment les décors opulents.* Glamourös: Michael Coorengel & Jean-Pierre Calvagrac lieben in ihrer Wohnung Opulenz.

56/57 Ensemble: the "Silver Room" combines the Baroque and the modern. *Effets : dans la « pièce argentée », le baroque et le moderne se côtoient.* Effektvoll: Im »Silbernen Zimmer« mischen die Besitzer ihre Vorlieben für Barockes und Modernes.

58/59 Bold colours: an Empire chaise-longue adorns the "Golden Room". *Oser la couleur : dans la « pièce dorée » le lit Empire repose sur un tapis de Verner Panton.* Mut zur Farbe: Die Empire-Liege im »Goldenen Zimmer« steht auf einem Verner-Panton-Teppich.

60/61 Sleep like an emperor: Napoleon is said to have once rested in this bed. *Le sommeil de l'Empereur : Napoléon Ier a dormi dans ce lit.* Schlafen wie ein Kaiser: In diesem Bett soll einst Napoleon gelegen haben.

62/63 Guarded by lions: Michael Coorengel & Jean-Pierre Calvagrac's bathtub. *Les lions veillent : la baignoire de Michael Coorengel & Jean-Pierre Calvagrac.* Von Löwen bewacht: die Badewanne von Michael Coorengel & Jean-Pierre Calvagrac.

64/65 Just as in Edith Piaf's day: her impresario Loulou Barrier lived here. *Comme au temps d'Edith Piaf : les canapés de son impresario Loulou Barrier, qui a vécu ici.* Wie zu Zeiten Edith Piafs: Hier lebte zuvor ihr Impresario Loulou Barrier.

66/67 Musical surroundings: Bertrand Burgalat preserves the original atmosphere of Barrier's apartment. *Tout pour la musique : Bertrand Burgalat a conservé l'ambiance de l'appartement de Barrier.* Musikalisch: Bertrand Burgalat wahrte das ursprüngliche Flair des Barrier-Apartments.

68/69 "Gisèle's Bra and Hair": Alexandre de Betak made this neon work for Victoria's Secret. *« Gisèle's Bra and Hair » : Alexandre de Betak a créé ce tableau au néon pour Victoria's Secret.* »Gisèle's Bra and Hair«: Dieses Neonwerk schuf Alexandre de Betak für Victoria's Secret.

70/71 Vis-à-vis: two sofas by Catherine Memmi furnish Alexandre de Betak's living room. *Vis-à-vis: deux canapés de Catherine Memmi se font face dans le séjour d'Alexandre de Betak.* Vis-à-vis: Im Wohnzimmer von Alexandre de Betak stehen zwei Sofas von Catherine Memmi.

72/73 Pride of place: two Louis XVI armchairs in Michelle & Yves Halard's salon. *Places d'honneur : deux fauteuils Louis XVI dans le salon de Michelle & Yves Halard.* Ehrenplätze: zwei orange bezogene Louis-XVI-Sessel im Salon von Michelle & Yves Halard.

74/75 Teamwork: an Yves Halard sofa, and above it a photo by his son François. *Esprit de famille : le canapé est une création d'Yves Halard et la photo de Capri de son fils François.* Teamwork: Yves Halard entwarf das Sofa – sein Sohn François machte das Foto auf Capri darüber.

76/77 The prize item: a neo-Gothic cabinet in the Halards' dining room. *Un joyau : une armoire néogothique trône dans la salle à manger mauve des Halard.* Schmuckstück: Im lilafarbenen Esszimmer der Halards thront ein neugotischer Schrank.

78/79 Creativity in the kitchen: Michelle Halard often works on her new fabric collections here. *Cuisine inspirante : Michelle Halard élabore souvent ici ses nouvelles collections de tissus.* Kreative Küche: Michelle Halard arbeitet hier oft an ihren neuen Stoffkollektionen.

80/81 Sleep in style: the female nude above the bed is by Bernard Dufour. *Nuits en rose : le nu féminin au-dessus du lit est de Bernard Dufour.* Stilvoll schlafen: Der weibliche Akt über dem Bett stammt von Bernard Dufour.

82/83 An imposing flight of steps: it leads to the showroom of fashion designer Anne Valérie Hash. *Impressionnant : l'escalier mène au showroom de la dessinatrice de mode Anne Valérie Hash.* Imposant: Die Treppe führt zum Showroom der Modedesignerin Anne Valérie Hash.

84/85 Splendour: in the main room, the Jurgen Bey "Light Shade Shade" chandelier provides lustre. *Fastueux décor : dans la salle principale, le lustre « Light Shade Shade » de Jurgen Bey.* Prunkvoll: Im Hauptraum sorgt der Kronleuchter von Jurgen Bey für Glanz.

86/87 "Marguery": the lettering is a reminder of the restaurant that was here in the 19th century. *« Marguery » : les lettres évoquent le restaurant du 19ᵉ siècle.* »Marguery«: Die Buchstaben am Kamin erinnern an das ehemalige Restaurant im 19. Jahrhundert.

88/89 Forming a semi-circle: Vladimir Kagan sofas in Cathy & Paolo Vedovi's living room. *En demi-cercle : canapés de Vladimir Kagan dans le séjour de Cathy et Paolo Vedovi.* Im Halbkreis: Vladimir-Kagan-Sofas beherrschen das Wohnzimmer von Cathy & Paolo Vedovi.

90/91 Study in blue: the Vedovis' Chinese-style ceramic stools and velvet couch. *L'heure bleue : les Vedovi ont marié le canapé avec quatre tabourets de style chinois.* Blaue Stunde: Die Vedovis haben die Samt-Couch mit vier Keramikhockern im China-Stil ergänzt.

92/93 Curvy: the spiral stair by Roger Tallon connects the Vedovis' kitchen with the roof garden. *Volée de marches : l'escalier de Roger Tallon relie la cuisine des Vedovi au toit-terrasse.* Schwungvoll: die Roger-Tallon-Wendeltreppe in der Küche der Vedovis.

94/95 A collector: Martin Hatebur has furnished his apartment with art and designer furniture. *Collectionneur : œuvres d'art et meubles design dans l'appartement de Martin Hatebur.* Sammler: Martin Hatebur hat sein Apartment mit Kunst und Designmöbeln eingerichtet.

96/97 Wall decoration: a work by Wool and two photographs by Gander behind the sofa. *Décoration murale : derrière le canapé, une œuvre de Wool et deux photographies de Gander.* Wandschmuck: Hinter dem Sofa hängen ein Werk von Wool und zwei Gander-Fotografien.

98/99 Brainwork: Martin Hatebur's desk was designed by Arne Vodder. *Travail cérébral : le bureau de Martin Hatebur a été conçu par Arne Vodder.* Kopfarbeit: Martin Hateburs Schreibtisch ist ein Entwurf von Arne Vodder.

100/101 A quiet place: Martin Hatebur's bedroom is on the upper floor of the duplex apartment. *Sobre et calme : la chambre à coucher de Martin Hatebur est au premier étage du duplex.* Ruhig: Das Schlafzimmer von Martin Hatebur liegt im Obergeschoss der Duplexwohnung.

102/103 In the limelight: a coffee table by Ron Arad below a Bouroullec Brothers lamp. *Mise en lumière : une table basse de Ron Arad sous une création des frères Bouroullec.* Ins rechte Licht gerückt: Ein Sofatisch von Ron Arad unter einer Lampe der Bouroullec-Brüder.

104/105 True fans: Patricia & Philippe Jousse chose Jean Prouvé for the dining room. *De vrais fans : Patricia et Philippe Jousse misent sur le design de Jean Prouvé.* Echte Fans: Patricia und Philippe Jousse setzen im Esszimmer auf Design von Jean Prouvé.

106/107 Made in 1939: the "Granipoli" table in the kitchen is also by Jean Prouvé. *Créée en 1939 : la table « Granipoli » dans la cuisine est aussi signée Jean Prouvé.* Aus dem Jahr 1939: Auch der »Granipoli«-Tisch in der Küche stammt von Jean Prouvé.

108/109 By Richard Jackson: "Accidents in Abstract Painting" in the Krzentowskis' home. *Signé Richard Jackson : « Accidents in Abstract Painting » chez les Krzentowski.* Von Richard Jackson: »Accidents in Abstract Painting« im Wohnzimmer der Krzentowskis.

110/111 A private art collection with a view of the Eiffel Tower: Clémence & Didier Krzentowski's home. *Œuvres d'art avec vue sur la tour Eiffel : chez Clémence et Didier Krzentowski.* Private Kunstsammlung mit Blick auf den Eiffelturm: bei Clémence & Didier Krzentowski.

112/113 Open wide: the photographic art in the Krzentowskis' dining room is by Barbara Kruger. *Dents carnassières : la photo ornant la salle à manger des Krzentowski est de Barbara Kruger.* Zähne zeigen: Die Fotoarbeit im Esszimmer der Krzentowskis ist von Barbara Kruger.

114/115 Open to the world: globes by Ange Leccia hangs from the bedroom ceiling. *Mis sous globes : une installation de sphères signée Ange Leccia dans la chambre à coucher.* Weltgewandt: An der Schlafzimmerdecke hängt eine Installation aus Globen von Ange Leccia.

116/117 Snappy: in Hubert Le Gall's hall a crocodile seems to be snapping a lamp. *À croquer : dans le couloir d'Hubert Le Gall, un crocodile semble s'attaquer à une lampe.* Mit Biss: Im Flur von Hubert Le Gall scheint ein Krokodil nach einer Leuchte zu schnappen.

118/119 Atelier d'artiste: Le Gall designed most of the furniture himself – including the "whale" armchair. *Atelier d'artiste : Le Gall a conçu presque tous ses meubles, dont le fauteuil-baleine.* Atelier d'artiste: Le Gall hat fast alle Möbel selbst entworfen.

120/121 A personal touch: the sofa and the "Sunset" shelves are Le Gall's own creations. *Très personnels : le canapé et les étagères « Sunset » sont aussi des créations de Le Gall.* Ganz persönlich: Auch das Sofa und »Sunset«-Regal sind Eigenkreationen von Le Gall.

122/123 Rustic charme: Le Gall's home is in the picturesque Cité des Fusains in Paris. *Comme à la campagne : la maison de Le Gall est située dans la Cité des Fusains.* Als wäre man auf dem Land: Le Galls Haus steht in der pittoresken Pariser Cité des Fusains.

124/125 Theatrical: Christian Louboutin's silver cabinet once a theatre prop. *Au théâtre : chez Christian Louboutin, l'armoire argentée était un meuble de scène.* Bühnentauglich: Der versilberte Schrank bei Christian Louboutin diente einst als Theaterrequisite.

126/127 Historic: Napoleon gave the armchair on the left to one of his generals. *Historique : le fauteuil rayé est un cadeau de Napoléon à l'un de ses généraux.* Geschichtsträchtig: Den Sessel links vom Kamin schenkte Napoleon einem seiner Generäle.

128/129 East meets West: Christian Louboutin's décor is truly international. *East meets West : Christian Louboutin aime les souvenirs de voyages.* East meets West: Christian Louboutin dekoriert seine Wohnung mit Souvenirs aus aller Welt.

130/131 A curiosity: carousels were once restored in Isabelle Puech and Benoît Jamin's loft. *Bizarre : autrefois on réparait des manèges dans le loft d'Isabelle Puech et de Benoît Jamin.* Kurios: Im Loft von Isabelle Puech und Benoît Jamin wurden früher Karussells restauriert.

132/133 Country style: Isabelle Puech and Benoît Jamin's kitchen. *Style rustique dans l'ancien bâtiment industriel : la cuisine d'Isabelle Puech et Benoît Jamin.* Country-Style im ehemaligen Industriebau: die Küche von Isabelle Puech und Benoît Jamin.

134/135 Velvet-covered: the two sofas are prototypes of designs by India Mahdavi. *Habillés de velours : les deux canapés sont des prototypes dessinés par India Mahdavi.* Mit Samt bezogen: Die beiden Sofas sind Prototypen der Entwürfe von India Mahdavi.

136/137 A collection of sofas and armchairs: the divan on the left is by Jean Prouvé. *Canapés et fauteuils : le lit de repos, à gauche, est un objet de Jean Prouvé.* Eine Sammlung von Sofas und Sesseln: Die Liege links ist ein Entwurf von Jean Prouvé.

138/139 Greetings from Scandinavia: an Arne Jacobsen chair in India Mahdavi's bedroom. *La Scandinavie au rendez-vous : une chaise Arne Jacobsen dans la chambre à coucher d'India Mahdavi.* Gruß aus Skandinavien: ein Arne-Jacobsen-Stuhl in India Mahdavis Schlafzimmer.

140/141 Paris as far as the eye can see: Sean McEvoy's living room commands breath-taking views. *Vue panoramique : le séjour de Sean McEvoy et ses vues époustouflantes.* Paris bis zum Horizont: Sean McEvoys Wohn-zimmer eröffnet atemberaubende Aussichten.

142/143 White cuboid: a five-metre-long bar made of Corian dominates the minimalist kitchen. *Cube blanc : un comptoir en Corian de cinq mètres de long domine la cuisine minima-liste.* Weißer Kubus: Die minimalistische Küche dominiert eine fünf Meter lange Theke aus Corian.

144/145 Fibreglass and steel: a Gabriel Vacher armchair in Sean McEvoy's bedroom. *Fibre de verre et acier : le fauteuil de la chambre de Sean McEvoy est signé Gabriel Vacher.* Aus Fiberglas und Stahl: Den Sessel in Sean McEvoys Schlafzimmer entwarf Gabriel Vacher.

146/147 Soft upholstery: guests at Rick Owens' PR showroom sit on armchairs of beaver fur. *Rembourrés : dans le PR-show-room de Rick Owens, les coussins des fauteuils sont en peau de castor.* Weich gepolstert: In Rick Owens PR-Showroom sitzen Gäste auf Biberfell-Sesseln.

148/149 Simplicity: steel and plywood furnishing by Rick Owens. *Sobre : l'extension date des années 1950, meubles en acier et contreplaqué de Rick Owens.* Schnörkellos: Der Anbau ist aus den 1950ern, das Mobiliar aus Stahl und Sperrholz von Rick Owens.

150/151 Archaic forms: "Gallic" chairs made of plywood in a Rick Owens office. *Formes archaïques : chaises « Gallic » en contreplaqué dans un bureau de Rick Owens.* Archaische Formen: »Gallic«-Stühle aus Sperrholz in einem Büroraum von Rick Owens.

152/153 Very sophisticated: Carine Roitfeld's sofas were designed by Charles Pfister for Knoll. *Très sophistiqués : les canapés de Carine Roitfeld ont été dessinés par Charles Pfister pour Knoll.* Sehr sophisticated: Carine Roitfelds Sofas wurden von Charles Pfister für Knoll entworfen.

154/155 From the architect's atelier: the table was once Le Corbusier's desk. *De l'atelier de Le Corbusier : la table servait de bureau à l'architecte.* Aus dem Atelier des Architekten: Die Tafel diente einst Le Corbusier als Schreibtisch.

156/157 Clarity: rooms by David Chipperfield including his own designs, such as this bed. *Lumineux : David Chipperfield a aussi décoré ces pièces avec ses propres créations, tel ce lit.* Klar: David Chipperfield gestaltete die Räume – auch mit eigenen Entwürfen wie diesem Bett.

158/159 Old splendour but modern: Rudolf Stingel's golden picture was painted in 2004. *Clin d'œil de l'ancien au moderne : le tableau doré de Rudolf Stingel a vu le jour en 2004.* Alter Glanz aus neuer Zeit: Rudolf Stingels goldenes Gemälde entstand im Jahr 2004.

160/161 Stylistic mix: an 18th-century urn on a Saarinen table in Gerald Schmorl's home. *Mariage de styles : une urne du 18ᵉ siècle sur une table Saarinen chez Gerald Schmorl.* Stilmix: eine antike Porzellanurne auf einem Saarinen-Tisch bei Gerald Schmorl.

"In the middle of the room was a big renaissance table, on it a lovely inkstand, and at one end of it note-books neatly arranged, the kind of note-books french children use, with pictures of earthquakes and explorations on the outside of them..."

Gertrude Stein, *The Autobiography of Alice B. Toklas*

« Au milieu de la pièce il y avait une grande table Renaissance et à une de ses extrémités des carnets bien rangés, le genre de carnets qu'utilisent les enfants français, avec des images de tremblements de terre et d'explorations sur le dessus...»

Gertrude Stein, *Autobiographie d'Alice B. Toklas*

»In der Mitte des Zimmers stand ein großer Renaissance-Tisch, und an einem Ende davon lagen ordentlich aufgereihte Notizbücher, wie sie französische Kinder verwenden, mit Bildern von Erdbeben und Entdeckungen auf dem Einband ...«

Gertrude Stein, *Autobiographie von Alice B. Toklas*

DETAILS

Détails   Details

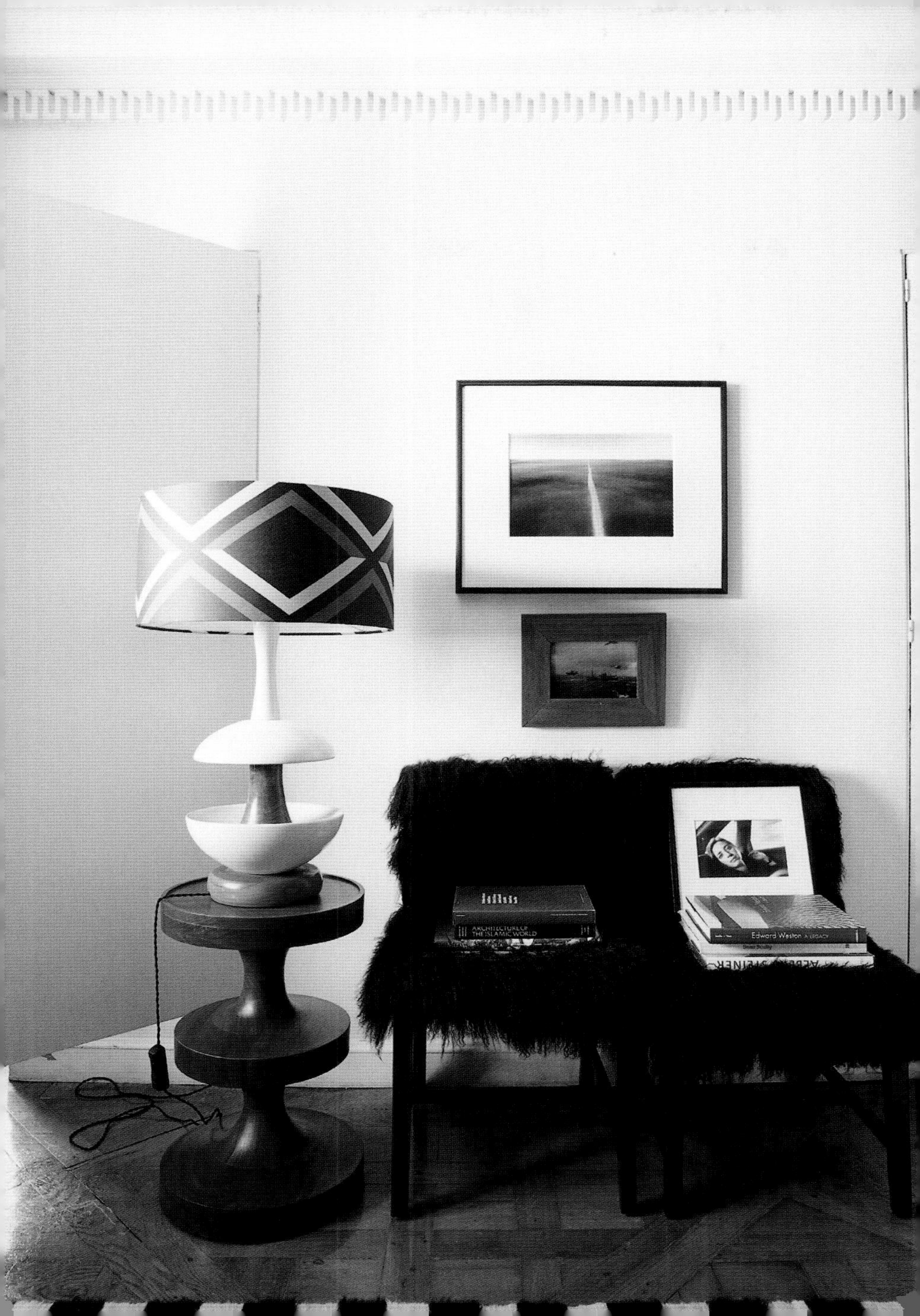
ARCHITECTURE OF
THE ISLAMIC WORLD
Edward Weston A LEGACY

171 Unmistakably French: a concierge's booth on Square des Batignolles. *Typiquement français : une loge de concierge au square des Batignolles.* Unverwechselbar französisch: eine Concierge-Loge an der Square des Batignolles.

172 Upwards: the staircase of an 18th-century villa – in the Marais. *Ascension : l'escalier d'un hôtel particulier du 18ᵉ siècle, au cœur du Marais.* Aufstrebend: Ein Treppenhaus aus dem 18. Jahrhundert im Marais.

173 A monument upside down: the Eiffel Tower reflected in a steel-and-lacquer table. *Effets de miroir : la tour Eiffel se reflète sur une table d'acier et de laque.* Ein Monument steht Kopf: Der Eiffelturm spiegelt sich in einem Tisch aus Stahl und Lack.

174 Fine items: sterling silver and nautilus shells on antique furniture. *Pièces de choix : argenterie et nautiles dans un buffet ancien.* Prachtexemplare: Sterlingsilber und Nautilusmuscheln auf einem antiken Büfett.

176 Reading matter: books on a bench of sapelli wood designed by India Mahdavi. *De quoi lire : une pile de livres sur un banc en bois de sapelli dessiné par India Mahdavi.* Lesestoff: Bücher auf einer Bank aus Sapelliholz, die India Mahdavi designt hat.

177 Open doors: a glimpse of Isabelle Puech and Benoît Jamin's cosy kitchen. *Portes ouvertes : la cuisine confortable d'Isabelle Puech et Benoît Jamin.* Offene Türen: Blick in die gemütliche Küche von Isabelle Puech und Benoît Jamin.

179 Sit or climb: the spiral stair leads to a wooden gallery. *Petites balades : l'escalier en colimaçon mène à une galerie en bois.* Perfekt für Streifzüge: Die Wendeltreppe führt zu einer Galerie aus Holz.

180 Golden letters the fireplace in Anne Valérie Hash's showroom. *Lettres d'or : initiales sur la cheminée du show-room d'Anne Valérie Hash.* Inschrift: Der Kamin im Showroom von Anne Valérie Hash ist mit goldenen Buchstaben verziert.

181 Inspiring: Anne Valérie Hash displays her fashion collections in fine surroundings. *Excentrique : Anne Valérie Hash présente ses collections dans un décor insolite.* Inspirierend: Anne Valérie Hashs Kollektion in extravagantem Ambiente.

183 A find: India Mahdavi discovered this lamp at a flea market. *Une trouvaille : India Mahdavi a découvert cette lampe aux Puces.* Fundstück: India Mahdavi entdeckte diese Lampe auf dem Flohmarkt.

184 High-class: the kitchen unit in Carine Roitfeld's apartment is coated with terrazzo cast resin. *Chic : chez Carine Roitfeld, le bloc-cuisine est enduit de résine coulée, style terrazzo.* Edel: der Küchenblock in Carine Roitfelds Wohnung.

185 Decorative: a Richard Avedon photo in Carine Roitfeld's apartment. *Noir et blanc : chez Carine Roitfeld, portrait de Penelope Tree par Richard Avedon.* Schmuckvoll: Penelope Trees Porträt von Richard Avedon bei Carine Roitfeld.

186 Glowing colours: Verner Panton's "Flower Pot" lamps illuminate Martin Hatebur's dining room. *Couleurs chaudes : les luminaires « Flower Pot » de Verner Panton éclairent la salle à manger de Martin Hatebur.* Leuchtende Farben: Verner

Pantons »Flower Pot«-Lampen erhellen das Esszimmer Martin Hateburs.

188 Creative space: in Rick Owens' apartment on Place du Palais Bourbon. *De la place pour créer : chez Rick Owens, place du Palais Bourbon.* Viel Platz für Kreativität: in Rick Owens Apartment an der Place du Palais Bourbon.

189 Ready to go: design by Rick Owens in PR rooms with lavish stucco decoration. *Ready to go : créations de Rick Owens dans des salles décorées de stucs.* Ready to go: Rick Owens zeigt seine Mode in reich mit Stuck verzierten PR-Räumen.

New Paris Interiors
Ed. Angelika Taschen / Texts: Ian
Phillips / Hardcover, 300 pp.
€ 29.99 / $ 39.99 / £ 24.99 /
¥ 5.900

TASCHEN's Paris
Ed. Angelika Taschen / Photos:
Vincent Knapp / Hardcover,
400 pp. / € 29.99 / $ 39.99 /
£ 24.99 / ¥ 5.900

Paris. Mon Amour
Jean-Claude Gautrand
Softcover, 240 pp. / € 9.99 /
$ 14.99 / £ 7.99 / ¥ 1.900

"Behind Paris's elegant exterior everything is allowed if it is different.
Angelika Taschen's selection of realms for living shows eclecticism
in all its guises – by people who know how to take lifestyle to the limit."
—*Elle Decoration*, Munich, on *New Paris Interiors*

"Buy them all and add some pleasure to your life."

60s Fashion
Ed. Jim Heimann

70s Fashion
Ed. Jim Heimann

African Style
Ed. Angelika Taschen

Alchemy & Mysticism
Alexander Roob

Architecture Now!
Ed. Philip Jodidio

Art Now
Eds. Burkhard Riemschneider,
Uta Grosenick

Atget's Paris
Ed. Hans Christian Adam

Bamboo Style
Ed. Angelika Taschen

**Barcelona,
Restaurants & More**
Ed. Angelika Taschen

**Barcelona,
Shops & More**
Ed. Angelika Taschen

Ingrid Bergman
Ed. Paul Duncan, Scott Eyman

Berlin Style
Ed. Angelika Taschen

Humphrey Bogart
Ed. Paul Duncan, James Ursini

Marlon Brando
Ed. Paul Duncan, F.X. Feeney

Brussels Style
Ed. Angelika Taschen

Cars of the 70s
Ed. Jim Heimann, Tony Thacker

Charlie Chaplin
Ed. Paul Duncan,
David Robinson

China Style
Ed. Angelika Taschen

Christmas
Ed. Jim Heimann, Steven Heller

James Dean
Ed. Paul Duncan, F.X. Feeney

Design Handbook
Charlotte & Peter Fiell

Design for the 21st Century
Eds. Charlotte & Peter Fiell

Design of the 20th Century
Eds. Charlotte & Peter Fiell

Devils
Gilles Néret

Marlene Dietrich
Ed. Paul Duncan, James Ursini

Robert Doisneau
Jean-Claude Gautrand

East German Design
Ralf Ulrich/Photos: Ernst Hedler

Clint Eastwood
Ed. Paul Duncan, Douglas
Keesey

Egypt Style
Ed. Angelika Taschen

Encyclopaedia Anatomica
Ed. Museo La Specola Florence

M.C. Escher

Fashion
Ed. The Kyoto Costume Institute

Fashion Now!
Eds. Terry Jones, Susie Rushton

Fruit
Ed. George Brookshaw,
Uta Pellgrü-Gagel

Greta Garbo
Ed. Paul Duncan, David
Robinson

HR Giger
HR Giger

Grand Tour
Harry Seidler

Cary Grant
Ed. Paul Duncan, F.X. Feeney

Graphic Design
Eds. Charlotte & Peter Fiell

Greece Style
Ed. Angelika Taschen

Halloween
Ed. Jim Heimann, Steven Heller

Havana Style
Ed. Angelika Taschen

Audrey Hepburn
Ed. Paul Duncan, F.X. Feeney

Katharine Hepburn
Ed. Paul Duncan, Alain Silver

Homo Art
Gilles Néret

Hot Rods
Ed. Coco Shinomiya, Tony
Thacker

Grace Kelly
Ed. Paul Duncan, Glenn Hopp

London, Restaurants & More
Ed. Angelika Taschen

London, Shops & More
Ed. Angelika Taschen

London Style
Ed. Angelika Taschen

Marx Brothers
Ed. Paul Duncan, Douglas
Keesey

Steve McQueen
Ed. Paul Duncan, Alain Silver

Mexico Style
Ed. Angelika Taschen

Miami Style
Ed. Angelika Taschen

Minimal Style
Ed. Angelika Taschen

Marilyn Monroe
Ed. Paul Duncan, F.X. Feeney

Morocco Style
Ed. Angelika Taschen

New York Style
Ed. Angelika Taschen

Paris Style
Ed. Angelika Taschen

Penguin
Frans Lanting

Pierre et Gilles
Eric Troncy

Provence Style
Ed. Angelika Taschen

Safari Style
Ed. Angelika Taschen

Seaside Style
Ed. Angelika Taschen

Signs
Ed. Julius Wiedeman

South African Style
Ed. Angelika Taschen

Starck
Philippe Starck

Surfing
Ed. Jim Heimann

Sweden Style
Ed. Angelika Taschen

Tattoos
Ed. Henk Schiffmacher

Tokyo Style
Ed. Angelika Taschen

Tuscany Style
Ed. Angelika Taschen

Valentines
Ed. Jim Heimann, Steven Heller

Web Design: Best Studios
Ed. Julius Wiedemann

Web Design: Best Studios 2
Ed. Julius Wiedemann

Web Design: E-Commerce
Ed. Julius Wiedemann

Web Design: Flash Sites
Ed. Julius Wiedemann

**Web Design: Interactive &
Games**
Ed. Julius Wiedemann

Web Design: Music Sites
Ed. Julius Wiedemann

Web Design: Video Sites
Ed. Julius Wiedemann

Web Design: Portfolios
Ed. Julius Wiedemann

Orson Welles
Ed. Paul Duncan, F.X. Feeney

Women Artists 20th & 21st Cent.
Ed. Uta Grosenick

ICONS